BOOKS BY LAURIE D. GRAHAM

Settler Education
Rove

Fast Commute

Laurie D. Graham

McClelland & Stewart

McClelland & Stewart and colophon are registered trademarks of Penguin Random House
Canada Limited.

Published simultaneously in the United States of America.

Library and Archives Canada Cataloguing in Publication data is available upon request.

ISBN: 978-0-7710-5197-5
ebook ISBN: 978-0-7710-5198-2

Book design by Andrew Roberts
Cover image: Laurie D. Graham
Typeset in Adobe Jenson by M&S, Toronto
Printed in Canada

McClelland & Stewart,
a division of Penguin Random House Canada Limited,
a Penguin Random House Company
www.penguinrandomhouse.ca

1 2 3 4 5   26 25 24 23 22

MIX
Paper from
responsible sources
FSC® C016245

Penguin
Random House
McCLELLAND & STEWART

The wish that the extinct reverse,
and the nearly gone be plucked from death
and managed, risks, in my mouth,
becoming a man with a chainsaw
on a plot the bank says he can do with what he wants

It's another hold around the neck of the land
that says I am and will be
and not the leaf on the branch
or the sap of the being

The idea of return is folly
without first understanding leaving,
how empires rose on its hastening,
every inch of territory pruned
to grow the desired, every life
movable, extinguishable, economic

And we visitors, we invaders, we small, individual specks
of death, we want the larger machines to pour their tailings, we want them
uprooting all life with their governmental limbs,
we want a fast commute morning and evening,
the terms of life rejigged for us and away from Earth
as council, balance as ethic,
the hard lessons of one's place within the whole

And now it's too late to pull
our trash from landfill and ocean, to say no
to plastic straws and pipeline expansions,
to maintain a slender innocence
as we turn away as largely
as the large machines keep turning toward

The trees at the feet of our parcels
bleed sap on our cars each yoyo spring
and we don't know why

The wasps are organizing in the eaves again
and we can't say our name for their species
before we exterminate

The girl is on the median with her hat out every morning,
the cars like a wide carpet around her,
and we haven't learned her name or where she's from

And we still keep songs of and for this place
locked in far-away museums

What do we know out our windows, carrying on
in spite of us? What do we tell ourselves
about the managed, shorn, tuneless expanses
that surely await us all?

Fast Commute

Banner, King Street, North Battleford, Saskatchewan, 1913: WE'RE YOUNG
BUT WE'RE AMBITIOUS

A foal flat on her side receiving a brand, while two other horses,
carrying the men who keep the ropes around her legs taut, recoil

A boy under thin-brimmed hat, scrabbling up corral logs, his face
full with all that will one day be subject to his iron

Rawhide postcard—*Moose Jaw Canada* and a cowboy with a gun—
addressed to Ben Crowther, Bradford, England, no missive

Aspen rustle, always aspen rustle, always saskatoon—*Belonging
to the Rose*, they write, *Related to the Apple*—I memorize
misâskwatômin, they say serviceberry, for the many ways it's
used, though I only see the birds at them, and the looks I get
when I pick from the pharmacy's landscaping

The tenor of care while the gig is to fix people's spelling errors, to engender future correction, a further cleaving of human from home

A Shipping Scene at Selkirk, Man., shore of the Red lined with lumber

Asphalt pathologies: the myth of unlimited growth,
turf hut to wood cabin to brick farmhouse

TB in the prisons and the schools,
structural, with an iron ear
as trauma turns to chemistry,
is inherited

~~recieve~~ *receive*, ~~stich~~ *stitch*, ~~your's~~ *yours*,
how these move the pencil, an urge
to render each visible invisible, while a
deeper urge says leave it be

Shortcuts through drywall neighbourhoods that won't make any map,
rudimentary graffiti, first swear words on a stained fence

The rivers commercial highways,
and the rails commercial highways,
and the roads commercial highways

What the verges return to untended: aspens thick together,
aspens sticky, aspens bright lime and rustling

White-tailed deer lifts head from alfalfa,
aims satellite ears at six lanes of paved artery,
humans each alone, dragging goods, encased in them.

HVAC drones of idling and revving
and earthmovers in a farmer's field,
in a new, interminable fog, spring arrived again

in winter, swallows feeding on what the machines kick up,
turkey vultures surveying the endless terrestrial renos
from very high above, the broken-armed maples smothered in vines,

coniferous stands salted, browning, Tyvek-threaded,
the roadkill fledging in long, wet grass,
the mist thick in each depression.

Bedroom windows higher than the sound barrier
as they churn more ground to make an on-ramp,
as they fill the hole with machines and grid up new rebar,

a man pressed between grids working a sparking tool,
belly of the earth exposed, outlet mall proliferating on his horizon,
creek secreted feet below the road, half-sheathed

in concrete, given a hard, straight course.
You could die of exposure
in ways you couldn't before.

Mechanic's/Mohawk Institute, established 1828
Kivalliq Hall, Marieval/Cowesess School, ended 1997
Your proximity to these first and last

Dufferin, Simcoe, Dundas, King, Queen, Victoria, so I never know
where I am and could be anywhere and this is heritage

A kistka and beeswax and an emptied egg, these grabbed-back materials
held in worsening sunrise, hand unsteady, the motions familiar,
the orange light, smell of wax bringing me closer, at risk
of being lost again, wage-earning like accelerant, my Toronto cough

Power poles, city blocks, grid layouts, irrigation systems,
blasts that burn predictable circles, demo crews promising
overnight completion, teetering commodity specs, new continents
of waste, the sod over a landfill that makes a mountain range

Billboard nailed to the evangelical church,
its parking lot like cooled lava

I do the math staring out a train window
as we pass a woman on a defunct track,
gazing through us to an instant of peace

Getting to know a river as a cure for loneliness,
the river swollen and unapproachable
after a season of record rainfall

Pigeon waltzes the trail on one foot and one little nub.
Mallards and their escaped domestic kin and the bright,
rasping horns of Canada geese in false spring, in glacier-
turquoise water. Hundreds and hundreds of sharps sinking
into the banks. Nests of clothes. Tents. Tarps. Broken trees
helped down the slope with chainsaws. Water rainbow-slicked.
The salt-spackled ground. The farmed transplants, the white-
bread crumbs. Up the bank: courthouse, hockey arena,
brutalist government tower, city museum, wind.

Down here, the fork in the river. The sacred.

Paint smudge. Shoeprints through a spill of yellow locust leaves.
Overhead, the jagged edges of a different leaf, larger, still green.

Forgetful of shape, pattern, name—English name or Latin name—
all I do is look at them, passive as television,

only reach out my hand when they're ailing or brightly hued.

Cars on the overpass, a drum with no beat, just frequency,
spraying detritus over the barricades, each stroke presumed

individual. The freeway held above the neighbourhood
like a trophy. Small yellow leaves swarming in side-road gusts.

Vegetable gardens beside a church, fences around the died-back.
Landscape fabric and stained mulch. The grass saturated,

the grass torn away along the artery, dandelion, clover, marigold
reflowering in approaching frost. The slough we pass on the way

to the liquor store. A juniper grey with berries,
flashing with waxwings. A rush of wind through squat maple

as the temperature drops swiftly.
All the while, engines along the raised vein.

Walking the sidewalks of an old suburb I do not know,
googling how to make pysanka dye out of all these black walnuts,

sidewalks on one side of the street, a childhood jack-o'-lantern
neighbourhood, the clouds frightening and rapid, low and sudden,

tall branches whipping, cars profuse along the thoroughfare,
a drone that forms in the south maybe, the on-ramps—

how the ear must have it start somewhere—

behind structures of cinder-block, behind exploding scarlet
Virginia creeper, exploding terrier on a rope in a yard, no beginning or ceasing,

the wildness right up to the wall with its shitty graffiti and holes cut
for firehoses at points blanked out by the flashing sides of trucks.

The angles of the roofs, the rain barrels, flower beds, fertilizer spreaders.
These versions of where I come from.

Knowledge of home in danger of becoming academic.

An empty can of energy drink under a sugar maple.
A black squirrel crossing critical thresholds:

roadwall, greenstrip, chainlink, trail, wooden fence, property.

Ubiquity of Tims cups. Buckthorn. Creeper. Confetti
of locust leaves reanimated by SUVs through the subdivision.

The bright yellow mush trails to nothing as the rain picks up again,
falls sideways.

Instead of ancestors, I have great-grandparents
subject to ad campaigns, who set down
in the broad middle of a new country,
the *why* rarely coming up

Made to pause at King and John
for a motorcade flying flags I can't name,
revolving offensive of cops on bikes, sirens
the only sound for a moment, while behind me
a crater dug for a glass tower collects bottles and bags,
becomes archaeological

Hrytsko Kitt brought his metal hammerhead,
he brought his wire mesh sieve.
On an old archived website,
I look at photos of Hrytsko Kitt's hammer and sieve

A bulldozed lot, once subject to a fleeting scent of profit,
regrows in a broken register, tar pails dumped
and rusting through, no clue the roof
where the tar was spread or where the pitch came from,
present-tense refuse and the goldenrod coming up around it

Imagine now a view out a train window as it slows,
approaching a station. The repeating city blocks, the uniform
trees European-derived, the comfort of replication,
the hard, cold material out of which all the buildings
are made, THE LAST BEST WEST, HOME FOR MILLIONS

White lines, their borders like breakage,
like faults on the ocean floor. To all those
killed by cars in the desert of downtown, the desert of exurb

When I speak of trees I'm one microbe
in a system of commerce, so as much as I can
I stay silent, and presented here, I reach outward—

Garbage bag ripped open in another dozed lot,
the food containers spread out and organized like candy
or entrails, and it's not clear whether
these substances will ever decompose

Hearing a child out the east window,
a train out the west window,
I write pysanky, я пишу писанки, *ya pyshoo pysanky*
in a hum of morning rush hour,
lines veering, asymmetric, trackless

And ahead of you, in the clearing, parting the low, wet,
web-threaded branches with your arms, you find them, lively
and emplaced, under bright grey sky and smell of recent rain,
arms curved like umbrellas, equal and green, in tableau,
and you've come to give them something, to return the gift.
So green. So happy to have been sent here.
Though you never do sit, you know now. You have
what they told you. You know what that dream was for.

I don't want to write it. I know the scene as home:
the oil refineries rising from poplars
overlooking the river, the tank farms downstream,
the offgassing from stacks painted like candy canes,
the manufactured cloud formations—
they treat these flames as eternal, eschewing the clean
for the cheap and the quick. I don't want this
tied to the trees or spoken aloud, this
inheritance, our confluence, our shame,
the windows of the houses on the opposite bank
observing the transfers, the neighbourhood park
that used to be the dump, and the quiet
of the river through each process, the banks
dropping away slowly, the river so large and old
it's thought both impervious and already dead,
but instead it's eroding the ground, and for good reason.

Civic pride blooms in gentrifying neighbourhoods,
children profligate, rooming house threatened,
WE'RE YOUNG BUT WE'RE AMBITIOUS

The feeling of moving remains
after the train comes to a stop,
and what sounds like ocean waves—
the idling motor defining our age

Geometry's assurances:
the eight-pointed star,
the pine tree's needles,
kistka's lines unending

Я пишу вірші, городи, писанки
Ya pyshoo veershi, horoadih, pysanky
I write poems, gardens, eggs

Sparrow clinging
to chimney chase
in impossible wind

Manitou Asinîy in the Royal Alberta Museum,
which we crawled all over on field trips.
They renamed it Iron Creek meteorite, obscured its meaning,
Manitou Asinîy powerful and not to be touched,
and what did we do by touching it

Cities joined, though separated by rivers,
cities twinned by growth, tension nested in the hyphen

The hardest dye to get to look right on the shell of the egg
is green, the symbol of hope.
My grandmother gathering crumbs
to the edge of the table as she spoke of other things

A terminal of people. Line for customs enormous.
We snake back and forth to take a turn at the head.

The game: to see what non-human life is
here and palpable, within range of the senses.

I go back to yesterday's pigeon
weaving through legs in the train station,

how that bird made it okay for the humans to look
at one another and smile and try to speak.

And the answer the brain gives is *air*, and what yeast is in it,
what organisms float on vapour among us.

A man in a blue checkered sport coat has hurt people,
it's plain to see.

I don't want this game to end with *air*.
Any trapped warbler quicker than my vision.

HUMAN CENTRED LUXURY printed on a billboard as big as a house.
The exhausted grip of the state. The checkpointing.

On the other side there's tarmac and airstrip
and pink pollution sunrise.

A miracle of snowy owls draw winter circuits overhead,
while through another wall of windows, a single sparrow

tries to solve how she, without
the tools of the maker, gets out of here.

Waiting for the ads on the airplane map to end
so you can see where over Gitchigami you are hurtling,
how you'll proceed over Thunder Bay,
breakwaters of ice foreshadowing where rock rises
above the level of water

Gypsum beds along the Grand River, the oil in the Thames,
flecks of gold in the North Saskatchewan

As long as the pysanky are written,
life will continue

Seeds in cold soil, early greens, early peas.
That smell is either brassica or pesticide

The white, weaponized self
making headlines every few days,
unfathomable to those who
haven't been subject to it,
the damage an explosion
through time, a fire gobbling oxygen

Carnage of the highway: raccoon, fox, cat, coyote, skunk, snake,
turtle, deer, gull, butterfly, crow, bee, dog, squirrel, uncountable
other insects

I have to turn away from the house and toward the fire,
slough the neon that tries to distinguish me from fuel,
gaze into that blue centre, try not to look away or will an explanation

Natal Day, 1915, children grouped according to age
in front of the hotel, which houses the bank, each class
hoisting a banner, pale men in dark suits all around

Sugar beets, an emptiness,
shoeless in the field

The bright beige dress of a sapling in a woodlot,
bent branches like a closed umbrella

The silver of moon, the rooming house, the cop car,
its cherries going, the wind, the man in the upstairs window
asserting obliviousness before a computer, who wrote
NATIVE in red chalk on the road during the street festival
and should be admired but is instead ignored, which is
better overall than receiving attention

The war monument and the climate-change photography
side by side in the public square,
hashtags organizing

Toxins dumped in rivers,
carried off and monetized

And the *quasi-religious ideas behind Arbor Day*, landscapes scraped
to treeless, the *inflexible grid* duplicates, the buildings same, craters of grids
deployed and deployed, the trees equidistant, transplants put down
in a spasm of public care, a donated truckload of mulch ready to suffocate them

Everyone was silent,
she says. Nobody spoke of
Holodomor and were encouraged
to lie about it and were threatened
when they wouldn't

My dad, with his brother, surveying in muck to the top
of the hip waders, somewhere in Saskatchewan,
I gotta do something else with my life

A five-year-old on a school bus wearing cat ears, crying,
staring hard at me as I wait at my stop

The sparrows at my feet,
the water bottles, the legacy—
a geyser erupts for the first time in decades,
spews a chronology of trash
catalogued by the archaeologists

The broad willow trunk. The weeping birch of childhood.
Towers piling up like a nightmare. Dense thickets
of monoculture. The railway, the roads, the walking trails
subverting natural north-south travel.
The bollards block the creek from view while we're driving.
Heavy machinery pressing new divots into the inside joke
of new roads. The creek split and unspooling
as the cars burn a bit more pitch to go get toilet paper,
the creek distended as surface roots push up asphalt
walking trails, the effort spray-painted orange for safety,
the path leading over a bridge to an abandoned lot's
checkers of weeds and concrete. Delivered by civic neglect
into trespass, culvert-minded, with polypropylene streamers
to approximate leaves in wind. A developer slaps his vinyl sign
on the side of a barn, his imagined new edge of a city.

No footpath, no worn shortcut across the park.
Bicycles sounding like trains across the wooden bridge.

Anything edible here I never did know.
The taste of grass in the mouth, the feeling

that doing this searching might kill me.

The birds soar high over the river.
The grasshoppers. The grass making a feeling

in the back of the throat.
Lone people, parked under trees.

Refinery giving way to ravine, giving way to
river. The refinery's chainlink lining one side of the trail.

Dragonfly hovering, the bank
receding, their chainlink in danger.

The smell of thistle, the sweetness of an open field under sun.
Sky and ground, half and half.

The roses, the raspberries, the human
scale. The massive rumble always there.

As you near the road,
you must turn toward it.

Stone barn, fuel cloud, chipmunk, dump truck,
dry rustle, goldenrod, milkweed, raspberry—

springing to life each morning ahistorical,
into excess of obliterated lot, deciphering

food on store shelves, lighting fires
that smoke from what's burning,

dismantling any tree, any squirm
of consciousness within one's human field—

fire hydrant, manure flinger, diesel smell,
man under tall cap disking sandy loam,

ducks across the storm pond,
snowmobile path, tractor path—

one day stripped to clay and laced with streets
named for British lieutenants

or for what's been dozed away—

walking trail, chainlink, fence board,
walk-out basement, facades of stone,

corn stalks, wet clay, crow call, asphalt crumble—
engines unrelenting across our horizons,

a minor second where the original
was a different mode entirely—

garden of scalloped concrete pads,
weed whacker through crabgrass,

the dips of the driveways, the barbecue covers,
back-alley cigarette butts—

a digger ripping up a structure,
yanking plumbing and support beams,

balanced on a carpet of limestone bricks,
on a carpet of river stones,

flag taped to digger's window,
brown seeds in silk through the demo site,

cement truck turning, set back from the action,
and the butterflies move differently,

in the shape of a question, hooking off
in another direction once the asking's done—

concrete washout, standing water,
AC units, parking structures,

workers' phobic dollar-store pranks,
rigs, busted streetlights, a loud wailing,

expletives thrown in the face of a panhandler,
wheat-paste advertising, landscapers, tar spillage,

tree sentences, place-making,
high, deep gusts today, dread—

Hawk precarious on a fencepost
as the grabbing machine
raises its fork to a tree
by the side of the highway,
the other tree, in its last
moments, next

Three men fish off a sandbar
below the freeway's evening rush hour

Semi trucks of cargo form a long stitch between guardrails
protecting industrial crops of corn, wheat, soy,
serial numbers on signs facing the thoroughfare.
Trapped in the living rooms of our vehicles,
our right feet hovering, loss presenting as impatience,
collecting in the tissue, in the fat

A net cast lengthwise around the egg.
Birch trunk of wax. Grass, crocuses,
though what I've written will come out in negative,
every line white once the wax is melted off.
The earth without its oceans is not round
like this. It's a knee joint hurtling through a window

To get to know the place you're living,
to feel the place you're from growing into your past,
a part of you receding
as you learn new plants and trees,
mute and teacherless,
before a backdrop of extinction

Knob and kettle lakes, glacial leavings, gravel pile, ice-chunk topology—
among the melted is where I was raised

They paved or buried the creek beds.
Moving past them all too fast to earn a paycheque,
upturned leaves in the periphery.
Smudging pencil lead with the finger to make smog.
A sense of profusion—the birdsong, the seeds—
but no longer profuse

The sky on the way home told me something,
its gold through clouds

A dream of asking them how they imagine
their great-grandchildren living in this place,
faces frozen in my mind like in the photos,
except for Baba's, her face I knew

Змія, *zmeeya*, the serpent, often wears a crown,
stalks the earth counting eggs, trapping evil spirits
in its spirals, protecting a household

A single dawn on a stationary bike
watching the commerce on the Fraser River,
log booms on the move,
tugs and barges, containers
floating by, under cover of near-darkness,
past a stern bust of Simon Fraser

A weed is a plant out of place, says the man on drive-time radio.
And vines choking trunks is the story of settlement,
the birches on the road home, their blood-rust at my feet,
the stain of their seeds across concrete

It might be farther out than I've realized,
or more various, numerous—
the bush, the marsh,
hacked down, filled in
everywhere I've made my home.
There might be no place I can live

Cormorant stands on a rock in the river,
holds out its wings in hot wind

We watch the sun ascend the cement factory.
We do it washed in magenta light

Aggregate conveyor pokes above the treeline at sunrise.
Silhouettes of crows perched in the silhouettes of trees,
fires not yet ripped through here. Sun orange and correctly

ascending over new mountains of developers' slag—
all the For Lease signs along the artery, all the Styrofoam castles
forming in the boonies. The signs won't stay up in the wind.

School buses bumping down the highway like apocalypse.
Earth mounded up, garbage gathering at the stumps of hills,
a canal of it grazing the houses' foundations.

Brownfield and a flash of fresh woodchips. Blue branches
and red ones and yellow ones in the sea of greys,
winter unending but constantly interrupted.

To cross this high over a creek, to stay that far away
and claim to live here. I had a dream about a return
of warmth, sudden and lively. Scratching a dog's ears

and getting a nuzzle in return. People gathered beside water.
A big five-armed birch. I woke to maples
bleeding sap on the sidewalks. I woke trying to tally

the loss in a clearcut, all that intelligence wiped out
for parcels of capitalist language. How I might also be
a tree ripped out, and the machinery, interrupting

any chance to dig in, to know somewhere.
The fury that builds whenever we pull up stakes.
And the need to do it, to follow the money. The relief I feel.

Geometric morning, grey glass twinkling to the apex
of my vision. I stare hard at the pigeons on the ledge.
The dead crow on the white line. The dead crow each day
on the white line turning to powder,
feathers disintegrating in cold rain.
Blue spruce in a concrete coffin barking with sparrows.
Cacophony of headlight, streetlight, lit sign,
double-paned, sliding, seeming to pass through one another.
Kids springing high from the alleys.
The busted bellows of the factories.
Birch disorganized, keening on choppy, warm clay.
Discarded wire fence indistinguishable
from raspberry cane in this light.
Remember your smell as you mixed with wind?
The scent of wind through your body?

I grow into each new place with scraps of elsewhere,
starting ignorant every few years, learning how
to set the expression and the posture, to make it look
like my knowledge possesses the possibility of depth,
and then, eventually, the body settled into its placement,
I become more like myself in that expression,
that posture. It's not the right way in. Its bedrock
is crudscape and monuments, the basic features any city shares.
Finally, here's a cone of chestnut flowers low enough
that I can smell it, learn if it has any scent.
Like the woman in the Costco who lives in a language
other than this one, trying to smell a sealed jug
of vinegar. And the looks she got. The revulsion.

Broken limbs on nearly all the trees along the rail path,
branches encased in ice one winter and snapped at the sockets,
the rail line ripped out and sodded over, then a patch of sod
pulled back to show a few remaining ties and a plaque erected,

the creek jangling along corrugated iron banks,
storm drains delivering salt and plastic with the melt and the rain,
grass pushed through any fissure, weeping willow trying to graze
the surface of the rusty water, sheared by the hard creek bottom.

The concrete gets tagged and greyed over and tagged, rough sketches
of the contours of hills, the tamped sand, the road crush,
the creek finding its course belowground. The concrete takes on
the striations of rock: ored, dark, shale-threaded,

alkaline. Groundwater corroding the rusted banks white.
An upturned paper plate, a sealed Tupperware with a sandwich in it.
Trees spilling over the embankment. Fat splat of drainage.
Dogging around feces to check on the state of the creek

before impending storm. A young willow pushed up through a fracture.
A man too old to be carrying all that steel through the fabrication yard
above. The drainage seems to scale an incline
before reaching the creek's concrete floor, its concrete channel.

Field of dead, waving goldenrod in an empty factory's parking lot.
The curled tongues of failed sod. The sickness of soil along the road.
Fresh sidewalks and the way the road crew stares down at me like cattle:
concerned, vacant, mawing.

The meteorologists are pleading with us
to keep checking back through the storm,
ice pellets making a carpet two, three inches thick,
this pale beach we walk on, this wind that passed
over the bodies of the lakes and the lakes that
froze it, the arctic sunk deep, meeting our cheeks,
gathering on us, this snake's rattle of weather,
this sandstorm of ice six inches deep and climbing,
these April showers.

That summer's birdcalls were new to you.
The guidebook's useless English syllables:

Drink your tea, Oh sweet canada canada canada.
You played your recordings for bird people

and non-bird people, stalked the songs in your dreams,
found the tones between keys on the piano.

One weekend there were men across the lake
straddling bikes, buffing chrome, squirting lighter fluid

on nightfall. In the morning, walking through
trailers and bikes and "Duke of Earl" on a loudspeaker,

your gaze thrown metres—eons—up the road,
you remembered that the birds are right to hide from you.

The beat of your shoes on gravel, on asphalt,
on sand. The horses you couldn't hear over the revving

showing ribs. The killdeer. The deer deer.
The wild carrot blooming. The wild grape.

The other society up in the trees
as you sat down alone at your table.

Groups of demo crew and road crew squatting on the steps
of a cladded-up building, heads tilted skyward
between hauls of smoke in this bomb scene of demolition,
the inside outside, the criss-crossed pipes in sand
below the sidewalk, a crumpled piece of paper
or a crumpled small black bird.
More workers up the road measuring out a crosswalk
with their own leg spans. Dudes in leathers gathered
in a parking lot to praise loudly
the beautiful unseasonable weather.

An unopened-eyed mouse writhes on basement concrete
after downpour. No sign of where it came from.
Dead sibling a foot away.
I toss them both into the flower bed.
A whole blink of life.

On rails, passengers must pause for freight, for lumber, oil,
crossovers fresh off the line and anonymous corrugated
freight containers, all of which should move us to place

our hands over our hearts, and maybe one day we'll be
forced to, but for now we'll wait, quietly, watching or not,
relishing stillness or not, the cars rumbling the ground,

endless, endless lumber and tank car, the odd grain hopper,
until it ends, gone, off west to be emptied or filled, and the
slow chug into motion after the freight passes makes it clear

that we're freight too, we're the secondary that justifies
the primary, that raw statehood, those trees, those tanks
of compressed life, and the renewed import of everything,

everything out the windows, it all practically carries a label:
fields of cut hay, swather's GPS windrows, rough
trench dug to direct the water, house boarded up, trailer

beside it graffitied—a fast assertion of shapes—the broken
branches of an old, lone weeping willow, rush-hour traffic
lined up the roads we cross, semi trucks carrying lumber and oil

and crossovers, and all that's in the spaces between these modes
of commerce, the dead brush, the garbage, the water in the dugout
and the life preserver, municipal art on the underpass walls

outlining untouched hills or the routes of rivers,
and the suburb sprouting up in the distance, the dry angles
and numbers of roofs, the lumber and the oil.

Beside an artificial lake, garbage collecting in its grates,
a pickup lays a patch at a slow speed, a novel blue cloud,
something akin to nostalgia—paintjobs, colours, curves,
reek of burning oil and unburned gas up and down Main Street,
the hoods up on some of the cars and the men peer in,
the hoods down on some and the men take pictures,
the hairdos on the women, the cans of pop with straws in them,
the lipstick on the straws.
Blue cloud, memento mori, farewell snarl.

A son writes his father's name in white paint on a red barn,
making sure to leave space to write *& family*,
transport trucks thick alongside, sheep and elevators,
a flock of solar panels, stakes up for the property lines.
Dozers scraping back the hectares, drawing nearer.
Thin wires of trucks pulling on and off the exit ramps.
Orange dust and daily engines, winter wheat emerging.

To understand that I am present here,

that I am sensed, that the soil feels me,

that the mourning dove knows my species

better than I know its species,

and with this understanding to start to hear—

Stands of windy birch tracing themselves like fingers

Birch spear wind-dark coniferous

Approaching rain a mouth of flies, of fireflies

The maple an hourglass, the trunk measuring

The trunk the conduit, the neck, the language

Crows in each treetop, parsing

The portable trailer under approaching cloud cover, its lattice of tire tracks

Words painting the overpasses—   *I love you   Grad 2015*

They'll cover it all in grey rectangles. They'll make this place a desert yet

        The threat of other life until you let your senses
        meet the moving form and do that hot work

I haven't yet talked to my garden. I've tended it gently, but I haven't
chosen the right words for it, haven't made my promise,
haven't written an egg for it

        The small dog stalks the yard,
        loses to moths and finches,
           chipmunks and houseflies

        Little difference between the billboard and the tag

I passed over train tracks seven times on the way to the market

Pigeon pressing down the wet grass.
Walks toward me thinking I have food,
away when it sees I have none

Downy woodpecker up a linden trunk.
A grey cloak around morning.
Chickadees seem to be shrinking,
chattering through the oak tree.
Crows in the field. Sparse alarm call from the robins.
Starlings at the top of the Norway maple,
their speech difficult, overpowering
once it takes root

Bull thistle, Plantago minor, mullein, comfrey, lungwort

I rise from my desk
and head out into the green

Quieter now, the engines, the roadwork, the generator,
cement truck, steamroller, pedestrian holler,

the chunking of bike gears, the colossal vents
of the curling rink, goose communication,

your slow stabs of thought, and a winter of crows
above, a system settling in over heated laces of concrete,

under darkening cradle of sky, the orange sodium triangles
snapping into place for the night,

the quivering of millions of flight feathers in wind,
the tangle of humans hurling themselves home

from their jobs under crows by the thousands, thick in the treetops.
You hop the fence of your humanity

to teem with the crisping choir of wings,
minds in such numbers, speckling the steel-grey sky

with their clamour and their planning,
and they can hear you, your exhalations,

your dumb wonder, your memory of magpie,
gopher hole, poplar scent, saskatoon,

what canola smells like, and Roundup, and oil refineries,
lodged in this form in this place coursing its own river,

which you want to get closer to but haven't
and can't yet, and the crows let you admit it.

Under their roiling dark bodies you're
nearly languageless.

The people around you look up and cower,
floor it past this receding stand of trees,

the roots with less and less to hold on to,
yet bird and human seem after the same thing:

warmth, safety in numbers, an unperturbed sleep.

Look how much farther the humans think
they need to travel to find it.

Ground fizzing and what sounds like artillery fire, three echoes.
Cornstalks and chunks of cob skittered into the ravine,
over the infill, over the boundary precipice.

Surface water trapped in sod, pooling in bootprints,
adding static to the whirr of a lone bird to the northwest.
The moving grass and the wind and a fly and a far stand of trees, whirring.

Trees cold, creaking, encircling, graffitied, human knives,
one tree smooth-skinned, one rough-skinned,
one half-smooth and half-rough standing inside the five-hundred-year-old

barricade, earthen, two-souled. A circle of raised earth
draped in impertinence of lawn.

Branch snap in the woods. Cannon fire, ducks displacing.
A single whirr to the north now, a red-bellied whirr.

At the gate, the biggest tree grown out of earthworks'
hump, roots let down all around, seed
accidental, singular, dead branches canopied above,

AF&JM carved twenty feet up.
Its roots are water, rolling in all directions.

The hard tack of earth once the soil's been cleared, its monochrome,
its sandstorms from gentle breezes, people in bulldozers hoping for rain
just like they did on workhorses, on their own feet in the field,
all that hoping in thin wisps: individual, private, corporate

Men in their caps against
the blue sky. How you could remain
as you were or grow better

Far-thinking tree farm on the bold prairie.
The last beset West, home for millions

The way the farmers speak in the NFB films
is where I come from and have nothing to do with,
it's mine and not mine at all

    threat propelling each syllable,
    thick tenor of self-preservation,

       fear behind the eyes
       tamped flat

To consort with ancients
　　　who say take what you can,
　　　　　throw the largest wake

The acrid scent of what's left

The grey of the parcel the best bareness
we can envision

The endless exchange of dirt
shipped from this municipal dugout
to that construction-site city
all in the service of

Daylighted creek flowing under the road,
jackhammers and small movers with small wheels,
canal-making, the intention of future calm,
but not now, now the unbearable creation noise,
　　　　　　　this civic scene

Further along the trail there's quiet,
birds, the tall of trees, rails that claim
to be active, the secret green valley,
old дідо, *deedoh*, gardening the land
        past his back fence.
            Along the verges life might thrive

A government owns a pipeline and its expansion,
owns its jobs and spills—does as Sir Sandford wanted—
takes on the margins of nation-building,
owns the irrevocable failed

            People gather around water,
            people gather on the divide between water
                            and thrown wake

Six men in the photo's frame, holding a calf down with their boots,
working the iron, or just sitting there watching it happen, a passive crouch
at the head of the animal—their faces aren't in the frame but you can bet
one of them's watching the calf's eyes as smoke rises from the iron on the
young animal's flesh, steam rising from the life of the calf in the cold air—

        I want to know what bleats at all their centres

Assuming new garden beds in the middle of the season in a new city
as I read about mass agriculturalization in Alberta,
learning a new set of frost dates and soil thinking,
going it alone with the weeds again, gathering what food's there,
ripping out the rest, how it's in the bones to panic, why
industrialization was born, the sure bet, the pacifier

Spruce, tamarack, poplar, birch

The need for drought,

the need for fire and flood

Constancy's the killer

Sorting, inventory-taking: creeping bellflower, orange trumpet
flower, wild grape, black raspberry, mint, bittersweet nightshade,
black-eyed Susan, stinging nettle, Virginia creeper, rhubarb,
what looks like caragana, lilac, Home Depot cedars poorly
planted, Manitoba maple, dog-strangling vine perhaps, lily of
the valley, those odorless perennial vines they call sweet peas,
hostas under full sun, ash

Helicopter's staccato drone in the distance as I bisect the egg,
draw dashes for water, the morning traffic cam, someone reading ads
up there for carpet-cleaners and discount pizza

Писанки, *pysanky*, derived from

писати, *pysaty*, meaning *to write*

Defeat stooking the fields
while writing wheat
on the egg to represent
a good harvest
and small circles
to represent seeds
and stars both

Torn trunk

                                exposed root
          scribble of twigs

Train lines turning to walking trails, turning civic,
callisthenic. Trees ripped instead of cut, wrenched out
with machinery. To tear apart a stand of black walnut
beside a fresh cord of two-by-fours. To make of this lot
a medical mall and this lot a food distributor

Sod house homesteaders, an adult and a child
in front of a house with a bushy, alive roof,
walls of earth, their smiles calm, rooting

Bugs like threads of smoke rise from the ditches.
Amisk Creek, Waskwei Creek, Old Water Tower Road.
Sea cans stacked two high along the rail line,
a temporary wall making north and south out of open fields.
Semis pulling tanks out of the Battle River Valley,
a procession of pickups collected behind them.
Bison a town symbol. The army base
next to their paddock. No discernible way in
except past a guardhouse. I'm like cattle,
a silhouette in failing light.

A braid of sweetgrass. One sparrow. A new danger of ticks.
Making lists: grasshopper, motorcycle blat, water tower,
dead mouse, sandbar in the river, markers fading,
highway drone, bird chatter, wind steady,
nest in the rafters of a shelter, quivering.
I won't go down the paved river trail—
those surfaces are what money gets you.
Up the valley, a garden of allotments and a campsite.
The garden speaking nêhiyawêwin,
words painted on stakes of wood.
The trucks in the campsite, the dust of the diamond.
The toolshed, the deer fence.
The paved path, the river's current.

And the girls walk out clean from the canola field,
the subdivision behind them.

At the crosswalk showing teeth
is how it's all been planned:

they're meant to smile at this moment in history,
stepping off the walking trail, cutting past the gas station.

They join their clean blond family for birthday dinner,
talking business, sales, Roundup for the weeds in the gravel driveway,

but not on the soil—making a point of never on the soil—
and when the appetizers come they all join hands

and pray, and the mother is obsessed with everyone's phones,
with who said what to whom and in what order,

and they're all real nice to one another,
right and good in their talk and their joking,

they bitch warmly about mean people at church,
for sure they're Humboldt Strong, can't tell if they're Justice for Colten—

The extractive machinery scrapes away
a wide, wide swath, an industrial-yard welcome.
Buildings poke out of the curved horizon,
appear as one in the distance,
a tasteful sci-fi of dread.
After a feeling of bush and home,
recalling the warmth as a child
of lights in the dark in the distance,
of the city appearing.

Crow in the poplar watching,
waiting for the call.
I wake early.
All the plants lining the path
have named themselves to me.
The dog stands devout
at the foot of the crow's tree.
In reliable dawn quiet
the mallards and geese
come out of the reeds with their young.

The cambium layer glows mustard,
one sign of an invader.

Berries small, hard, still green.
When they turn purple they make a green dye,

on the eggshell pale chartreuse,
the shade of grass not yet finding sun.

Buckthorn keeps repeating the reason for its arrival:
to stop wind after clearcut, to be vigorous and look like home.

The idea was for it to be predictable. Roots changing
soil, building up the familiar, suppressing what's there.

The saw is rusty and goes through that bright skin
roughly. I had no thoughts for the buckthorn

until sitting down to write this. In pieces in a bin,
it must have felt something, to be hacked apart.

Coyotes howl in the farmyards. Red squirrels trim
the pink of evening and the cicadas broadcast.

The mosquitoes try to learn the insides of my ears.
Property lines faltering, sod laid all the way to the water

faltering. The western half of the country has caught fire;
they think it'll burn all summer.

I check the branches of the saskatoons after the waxwings feast.
I keep returning in my mind to the towns of my parents and grandparents.

The mosquitoes browse. The loon is convivial and far away.

The spider's tendril flies from the edge of the bowl in firelight.
Thunderheads spin the far dark.

Cattle and coyote and the chest hurling itself up the road,
down the road, stuttering back to the fire.

Blood in the ears each night like a train.
Mosquitoes dancing in search of.

Thunder quakes through water and limestone, rings the lake
and degrades. At first light the birds

will confabulate a forest. Red mite crossing the back
of a ladybug that circles the rim of the bowl.

The longing, the lively, the study. What you do in trees, how you breathe here, how you know, why you have knowledge and what mode you have, what that knowing might mean here, for you, for the tree, why is this, the ground composition, what kind of soil, and again what kind, what do you tell people about yourself and where you live and where you come from, what do they understand, what are you doing here, why here, how long are you staying, are you putting down roots here, do you think this is where you'll settle, are you there now, are you Ontarian, is that home, does it feel like home, are you going home this summer, are you going on any trips, do you think you'll get some time to relax, what you tell people about yourself and all the places your friends live and how hard each time, how lonely, to start over again, and how digging in and staying put is impossible when you don't have money, and how a home needs to be built from something, and how you can't always build from what you've inherited, which means you have to listen better than you've been taught, which means that listening can be your home.

In the hills, aspiring.
The songs of combustion
don't fill each day.
I walk home mostly alone,
which is of course untrue
but feels like a thinning.
The hard dye of late summer
on my fingers, staining
not as long as you might think.

Ants tend their larvae underneath the rocks
around the fire where I cook my dinner
and warm myself into night, sending smoke
through my clothes, down my throat,
and off around the lake. The winds are
circular here. The island is circular.
All roads lead you back to the start.
The ants writhe under their one slab of rock.

Sun and leafmold and a form of calm, a way of knowing.
Branch fix. Undergrowth. My hand moving mosquitoes
off your scent, your exhalations, for the moment.
The emissions of our breathing. Birds flush through the gut
of aspen city, the mule deer browsing, the blackfly swarm
of memory, a sandhill crane, a high flock of them, a wren's
complex song. Aspen rustle, always aspen rustle, always saskatoon—

How trunks ice up on one side,
shimmering bronze in late sunrise.

The silence of hard freeze.
The hawk, the grader.

The strength
of oak leaves. The strength

of sparrows. Carrying yourself
around. How the hawk looks like

a song sparrow
in the top of the tree.

The long shadow of branches
lofting sun into morning sky,

the wide sweep of arms mapped
over forest floor, the light returning,

refracting breath and the belief,
somehow new each time,

that warmth will return, does return,
that the arms of trees will keep

lofting light above us a bit higher
each day, that in the depths

of coldest night there still exists
the promise of summer.

In the rounder pool of morning,
when birds stop speaking.

In the swallowing of summer, the light
descending trees and browning them.

In the thick of your body carrying
you into newness of cold.

Listen for the mouse, its burrowing,
its foundation path, its tasting

the depths of coming winter.
Be this mouse, if you can.

Feel where the warmth resides.
Make home of the larger forgetting.

Pages 5, 6, 19, 23, and 56 borrow imagery and idea from *The Last Best West: Glimpses of the Prairie Provinces from the Golden Age of Postcards* by Ken Tingley (University of Alberta Press, 2011), which draws from the Bruce Peel Special Collections Library at the University of Alberta (peel.library. ualberta.ca).

Page 9: A kistka is the tool used to "write" in melted beeswax on eggs in the Ukrainian tradition. It's a pen-like tool with a hopper for the wax that ends in a pinhole funnel, which is the point you draw with.

The "old archived website" showing Hrytsko Kitt's tools on page 14, as well as a poster advertisement containing the words "THE LAST BEST WEST, HOME FOR MILLIONS" on page 15, can be found on *The Last Best West: Advertising for Immigrants to Western Canada, 1870–1930*, Canadian Museum of History (historymuseum.ca).

Italicized words and ideas on page 24 come from *The Urban Prairie* by Dan Ring (Mendel Art Gallery & Fifth House Publishers, 1993).

The woman speaking on page 25 about the silence around Holodomor comes from the film *Hunger For Truth: The Rhea Clyman Story*, part of the Holodomor National Awareness Tour, which has toured the country visiting schools and museums since 2016 (holodomortour.ca).

Page 32: It was Ed Lawrence who said "A weed is a plant out of place" in his gardening segment on CBC Radio's *Ontario Today*.

The branding imagery on page 54 comes from the photograph "Lone Tree branding, Canuck, 1957," in *Everett Baker's Saskatchewan* by Bill Waiser (Fifth House, 2007).

ACKNOWLEDGEMENTS

I send my gratitude to Treaty 6 territory, the Haldimand Tract, London Township Treaty territory, Toronto Purchase Treaty territory, and Treaty 20 territory, all of which have given me life and are the reason I wrote this poem.

Many thanks to Jan Zwicky, Pamela Mordecai, Tanis MacDonald, Madhur Anand, Sarah Tolmie, and Dionne Brand, key readers all. Thanks to Tim Lilburn, Yasuko Thanh, and my family for conversations that sent me off in crucial directions. And дуже дякую to my great-auntie Onorka Mudryk for teaching me the Ukrainian word for *garden*. The Al Purdy A-Frame Association allowed me to go a bit sideways and write the end of this book first, and *Brick* magazine occasioned the commutes on buses and trains that let me work out the beginning and the middle. The Canada Council for the Arts, the Ontario Arts Council, and the Region of Waterloo Arts Fund gave their financial support to this project. And though they don't often appear on the page, Mark Jull and Ruby were with me through much of this.

Versions of poems and pages from *Fast Commute* were previously published in *The VIDA Review*, *The Literary Review of Canada*, *The New Quarterly*, *Arc*, *Vallum*, *The Goose*, *The Dalhousie Review*, *The Scales Project*, and on the CBC Books website; in the anthologies *Watch Your Head: Writers and Artists Respond to the Climate Crisis* (Coach House Books, 2020), *Rising Tides: Reflections for Climate Changing Times* (Caitlin Press, 2019), *Sweet Water: Poems for the Watersheds* (Caitlin Press, 2020), and the University of Saskatchewan MFA Variety Show; and in the art chapbook project *The Larger Forgetting*, a collaboration with painter Amanda Rhodenizer that first showed at Open Sesame in Kitchener. Selections from *Fast Commute* were also finalists for *The Malahat Review*'s Long Poem Prize and the CBC Poetry Prize.

LAURIE D. GRAHAM grew up in Treaty 6 territory (Sherwood Park, Alberta). She currently lives in Nogojiwanong, in the territory of the Mississauga Anishinaabeg (Peterborough, Ontario), where she is a writer, an editor, and the publisher of *Brick* magazine. Her first book, *Rove*, was shortlisted for the Gerald Lampert Memorial Award for best first book of poetry in Canada. Her second book, *Settler Education*, was a finalist for Ontario's Trillium Award for Poetry. Her poetry has been shortlisted for the CBC Poetry Prize, won the Thomas Morton Poetry Prize, and appeared in the *Best Canadian Poetry* anthology. Laurie's maternal family comes from around Derwent, Alberta, by way of Ukraine and Poland, and her paternal family comes from around Semans, Saskatchewan, by way of Northern Ireland and Scotland. She has about a century of history in Canada.